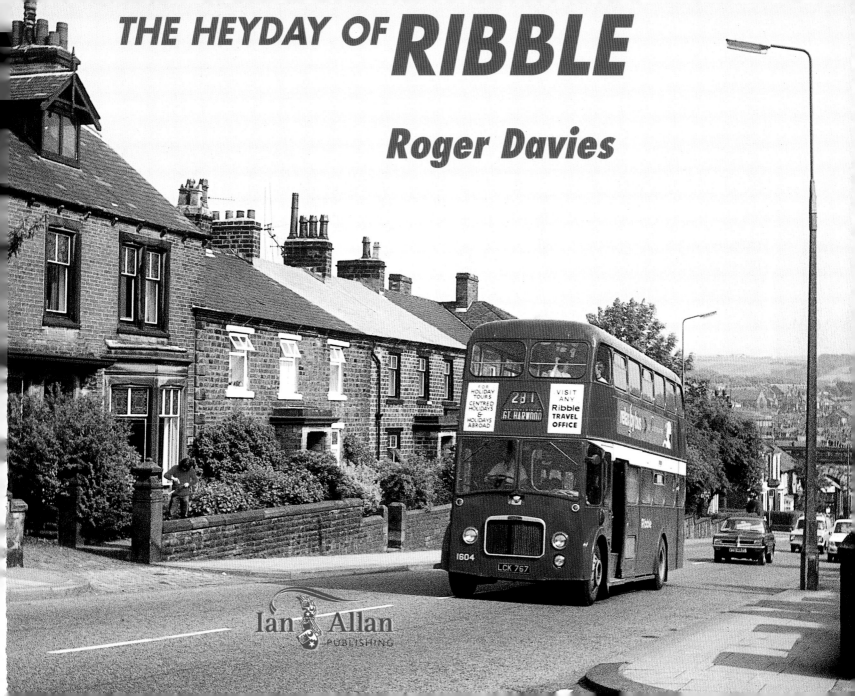

THE HEYDAY OF RIBBLE

Roger Davies

Ian Allan
PUBLISHING

Introduction

First published 2007

ISBN (10) 0 7110 3208 4
ISBN (13) 978 0 7110 3208 8

Published by Ian Allan Publishing

an imprint of Ian Allan Publishing Ltd, Hersham Surrey, KT12 4RG
Printed by Ian Allan Printing Ltd, Hersham Surrey, KT12 4RG

Code: 0711/B1

Visit the Ian Allan Publishing website at www.ianallanpublishing.com

How on Earth do you determine a heyday for something like the mighty Ribble? I had enough trouble defining the Glory Days! Anyway, let's have a go; let's revisit the great days of a fabulous institution that touched so many people's lives — 'The Ribble'.

Maybe the heyday was the 1920s, with the great expansion led by the dynamic Major H. E. Hickmott, founder of the company as we know it and a bus-industry giant, spreading the company from humble beginnings in Preston to stretch from the Mersey to the Scottish border? Perhaps it reflected the skill with which countless other companies were bought, assessed and absorbed into Ribble? Maybe it came with the establishment of that powerhouse (and bureaucratic centre), the Head Office in suburban Preston known always as just 'Frenchwood'? Perhaps it described the embracing of the new rules after the 1930 Traffic Act, the daily appearances in traffic court, the myriad of joint workings with huge numbers of other bus and coach operators? Then came the brave and sterling efforts put in by all staff during World War 2, when the company served vital industries, often under difficult and dangerous circumstances. After the war came the stunning 'White Lady' double-deck coaches, the appearance of which amongst the decimated streets of Lancashire must have lifted many a heart and demonstrated great optimism for the future. Or perhaps it followed the expansion of express services throughout the land and the company's constant battles to promote the interests of coach passengers? And the embracing of the new motorway network, the introduction of day trips over 300 miles in length as the M6, in particular, grew. Yes, yes, we are getting somewhere: this latter culminated in a heyday, the operation from 1960 of the 'Gay Hostess' double-deck coaches — a peak of British coaching history and a testament to Ribble engineering. And *what* engineering! Not only did it ensure a splendidly maintained fleet, but it also influenced the bus-building industry through the company's close association with Leyland Motors. Would there have been an underfloor-engined Leyland single-deck bus so soon had it not been for Ribble? What about the development of trend-setting 72-seater forward-entrance double-deckers in 1957, when London was still messing about planning to put 64-seat rear-entrance things on the road? And then the early adoption of first-generation rear-engined double-deckers (and subsequent rejection of same as not yet up to scratch)? Oh yes, Ribble certainly had its influence! Then there was the administrative system of individual running sheets, unique to the company ('everyone else is out of line then'), and the remarkable depot-identification scheme whereby each depot had a two-letter code used on all paperwork and carried on a third tax disc in all vehicles. Then there were the magnificent coach tours, pioneering coach-air holidays, and a chain of booking offices throughout the North West, where all travel requirements could be met. Ribble had its own architect with his own department, and magnificent bus depots and stations grew up in Aintree, Liverpool and all over the patch. Perhaps the heyday came in the Horace Bottomley years, when, as General Manager, he was a father figure to this massive company, and its staff were one big family. Yes, there was the marvellous 'Ribble Family', the huge social whirl that brought company people and their families together, be it for sports fixtures, safe-driving awards (2,237 in 1957 alone), providing digs for fellow employees or sharing the roof of a Royal Tiger to pick damsons in the Lyth valley. Indeed, in the 1930s the annual Ribble sports presentations, with their associated Beauty Queen contests, were the largest events staged at the Winter Gardens in Blackpool, being attended by more than 5,000 people. In the 1960s these events still were able to attract major pop groups, such as the Hollies at the height of their fame. And there was the size. In 1956, at its peak, Ribble carried 215,648,878 passengers, a figure that was probably (and I'm not going to check, so don't be picky) greater than the population of the USA at the time. Breathtaking. Then there was the sheer scale and diversity of Ribble's operating area. If you approached it from the north you came across the buses in the northern suburbs of Carlisle, a 665 at Kingstown (now near the home of Eddie Stobart Transport) or a 666 at Lowry Hill ('Lousy Hill' to crews!). If you crept into England through the back roads you came upon Ribble even further north, at Noblestown, on the 686 route. If you took the quick way south, the M6 (arguably Ribble's personal motorway), it wasn't until you crossed the Thelwall viaduct over the Manchester Ship Canal some 75 miles later that you could say you had truly left Ribble's territory in the North West. (Oh heck, I've missed out Barrow!) Even in its state-owned National Bus Company days Ribble still exuded charisma, being known in certain quarters as the 'Über Alles' bus company! Maybe the heyday was the day I turned up for a retirement presentation in a sports jacket and non-matching trousers, to be taken aside and quietly advised that, at Ribble, we wore suits.

So how, I ask you, do you choose a heyday from that lot?

In reality this pleasant task was constrained by the availability of colour pictures. So this isn't a collection of shots of all the types of buses operated; in fact there are far too many MCW Orion-bodied Leyland PD2s for comfort! Mind you, I liked Ribble's, and I always associate this type of bus with the company, despite there only being 75 of them. I recall seeing lots of them circled to form a compound for scrap metal at a breaker's near Barnsley, but let's not dwell on that. And I'm not being pedantic about the correct shade of red carried by the vehicles, Ribble red. Many of these shots have got it wrong, but no matter; take them for what they are, and, sacrilege though it may be to suggest such a thing, the bus is a bit secondary! Hopefully those with no particular interest in buses will find something to stir memories here. And for those who are not Ribble *aficionados*, hopefully you too will find scenes that bring back memories of areas you knew. Notice the absence of street furniture, the lack of traffic and the dominance of the bus. Days not that long ago, but an age away in terms of social history.

So here it is, a humble enough effort to try and capture the essence of what was, without doubt, one of the UK's finest bus and coach companies. Who's to say what summed up the heyday? Certainly many of these pictures capture it, but those days are gone. A little of Ribble survives: the sign for the staff club — the 'Ribble '72 Club' — still hangs in Lowther Street, Kendal, and Stuart Maconie, in his book *Pies and Prejudice*, refers to Ribble buses in Skelmersdale as if they are still there. Thankfully, they still live strongly in the collective memory of the Ribble 'Family', and long may that continue. Hopefully this book will play its part.

Roger Davies
Leeds
September 2007

Acknowledgements
As ever, thanks go to everyone who has been enthusiastically supportive of this venture; the magic of Ribble is still strong. The mistakes (again, as always!) are all mine. But this is essentially a picture book, and without the photographers it would not have been possible. So, my sincere thanks to David A. Powell (again!), Anthony Drury, Richard Mellor (at last!), Peter Yates, John Howie, Alan Haydock and, last but by no means least, Monica Richardson, who helped me so much by making available the fabulous national treasure that is Photobus — a wonderful legacy of her late husband, Arnold.

Readers may wish to know that the Ribble Enthusiasts' Club is still very active and can be contacted at 11 Regent Road, Walton le Dale, Preston, PR5 4QA, while the Ribble Vehicle Preservation Trust has many Ribble vehicles under restoration and can be reached online at www.rvpt.org.

Left: If you go back (no, don't) to all that guff in the Introduction you'll recall me going on about how difficult it is to pick out the heyday of Ribble. No it isn't — this picture does it all! Look at the pride, the character oozing from a classic Ribble type — and just look at its condition! By the time it was photographed in Grange-over-Sands in March 1970 'Red Setter' 219 was already three years old, but you simply can't tell. A Marshall-bodied Leopard, it was fitted with an air-shift gearbox so, for the purist, might not, on reflection, qualify as a 'Red Setter'. Newby Bridge, whither it is headed, was a connecting point at the lower end of Lake Windermere at which buses from Kendal, Ambleside and Windermere all linked up with the comprehensive network serving the Grange peninsula — an area nowadays rejoicing in the name of 'Lakeland Peninsulas' (and with flash double-deck buses). By the way, as 'mere' is Cumbrian for 'lake', 'Lake Windermere' (the only one of the Lakes actually referred to as 'Lake ___') translates as 'Lake Winderlake' …
Arnold Richardson / Photobus

Above: A busy scene in Wigan *c*1970, with typical Ribble types mixing with Corporation buses. Semi-lowbridge Atlantean 1680, the last of Ribble's first batch of such things, heads off for Preston on a 125 via Bamber Bridge, Chorley, Coppull and Standish — a route, unusually in this area, joint with no-one! *David A. Powell*

5

The Ramblers' Association have rambled off, leaving their modes of conveyance, Standerwick Leopard/Plaxton 733S and Ribble Leopard/Harrington 715, parked amongst picnickers at Arnside in 1971. A passing old lady considers the merits of the two types of rear-end styling applied to Ribble's first 36ft-long coaches. In the distance is Grange-over-Sands — beyond the waters of Morecambe Bay, said to flow in faster than galloping horses, but I think the coaches are OK. An enquiry to Thwaite's Brewery when I fancied a pint of their finest elicited the information that the Crown Hotel here was their most northerly outlet. Whether it still is I know not, but the beer was mighty fine. *David A. Powell*

"Eh up, our Margaret! Wi' decent livery and an exposed radiator, yon MCW Orion can be a reet fine-looking motor." "Never mind that, Harry — if you think, after refusing me a nice pot o' them whelks at that lovely caravan back there, you are going to get a pint of Magee's at that there Bourne Arms, you've another think coming!" PD2 1381 enters Knott End on Sea in September 1969.
Arnold Richardson / Photobus

Left: The 50 Saunders-Roe-bodied Tiger Cubs of 1953/4 were interesting in having been bodied on Anglesey. They were pretty classy, modern-looking buses too and introduced one-man operation at Ribble from 1958, being, in all honesty, the saviour of many routes. They were the start; other single-deck types were soon converted before purpose-built OMO buses were delivered. This lovely shot of 452 is cheating really; it was taken at the 2006 Leyland gathering, the bus being preserved by the splendid Ribble Vehicle Preservation Trust. But it is irresistible! *Alan Haydock*

Below: This atmospheric shot at Ormskirk early in 1967 features Olympic 268, which has ventured south to brave Lancashire's stone setts for its last few months of Ribble service. Throughout their lives these buses were more usually associated with the Lake District. This example went on to work for a while with a contractor. No 1486, a 1956 PD2/MCW, still had three years to go with Ribble before (probably) ending up in the circle of wagons to which reference is made in the Introduction. It was one of the last batch of rear-entrance buses purchased by Ribble. *John Howie*

Right: Once synonymous with Ribble were the all-Leyland Royal Tiger buses, 110 of which were delivered in 1951 to withstand the effects of Lancashire's stone setts. The standard Leyland design was modified for Ribble requirements including the incorporation of an angled windscreen, to cut down glare. And just look at the fleetname moulding on the front! By 1967, when 328 was photographed at Aughton near Ormskirk, it was one of only four left. Although modified in 1963 for one-man operation it is carrying a driver, a conductor and an inspector — rather high staff costs for a 44-seater! *John Howie*

Right: Now, we may as well get this out in the open. NBC's poppy red was not a 'heyday' colour at all and compared with Ribble's deep red was ... well, just plain naff. But Ribble managed to continue its heyday deep into NBC days, not only through its charisma but also by buying 104 of these magnificent machines, Park Royal-bodied Leyland Atlantean AN68s, and staving off too many Bristol VRTs. Just imagine how magnificent they would have looked in proper livery. Still, we can't do that, so here's 1363 of 1974 crossing the railway station bridge in Preston on a service theoretically joint with Preston Corporation but usually worked by Ribble. *Anthony Drury*

The 'Red Setter' Leopards represented another significant economy in that with 53 seats they matched the capacity of a 1952 double-decker. As things got worse financially for Ribble (and the industry in general) during the 1960s one-man operation became the saviour of many a route. Ribble started the process in 1958 using 44-seat single-deckers drawn from the supply of Tiger Cubs (one of which can be seen in the background), Royal Tigers and Olympics. However, when these 53-seaters were suggested the unions insisted they be downseated to 45 (Ribble not being alone in facing this request), so, from 1966 until 1972, a number operated in this form. One such was 598, a Weymann-bodied example, seen about to leave Blackburn for Preston via Mellor Brook on Ribble's lowest numbered route. Mind you, you'd have to have known where it was going.
John Howie

The delightful Eden Valley, east of Penrith and host to some of the calmer stretches of the Settle–Carlisle railway line, was home to some of Ribble's most deeply rural routes. Kirkoswald — KO to everyone except Ribble, which in its unique depot identification system referred to the outstation there as BQ — was home to three buses that served many of these routes. Near KO, crossing the Eden at Lazonby in November 1970, is 'little Leopard' 664. There were 55 of these pretty little 44-seater buses built in 1966, but 'little' was their problem, and it was difficult to find homes for them all. Still, apart from two that were burnt out they all put in a decent innings, and this one ended up as Ribble's mobile office for the Market Analysis Project that NBC introduced throughout its subsidiaries in the late 1970s and early '80s.
Arnold Richardson / Photobus

Perhaps in recognition of the unions' reluctance to accept more than 45 seats in a one-man bus, for 1966 Ribble ordered 55 short Leopards — soon known as 'little Leopards' (or even Leopard Cubs!) — with only 44 seats. The reduction of one was to allow the provision of a reversing window in the rear, this feature being shown in the second picture. Many of the rural routes for which these buses were intended necessitated reversing, so it was a sound idea. Sadly, with the demise of rather a lot of these routes, 44 seats just wasn't enough, and these delightful buses, with semi-automatic gearboxes (and thus really nice to drive), became a bit of a pain to allocate. These rare and fascinating pictures show 634 in its first week in service, operating a regular private hire to a small trading estate in Maghull not too far from its base in Ormskirk. The destination should probably be 'Private' rather than 'Preston'! *John Howie (both)*

Talk about heyday! Standerwick 'Gay Hostess' Atlantean 34, a Blackpool motor, heads for home as it zooms along the M6 (arguably its spiritual home), passing Charnock Richard services in a scene that sums up the futuristic view of the 1960s. These magnificent trail-blazing coaches were initially shared between Ribble and Standerwick, a name Ribble had wisely retained for its quality associations since takeover in 1932. The Ribble ones were used on routes to Bristol and the West Country, running on ordinary roads on which their speed and air suspension were not fully appreciated. Within a few years all were concentrated on motorway services under the Standerwick and (from 1968) Scout names. *David A. Powell*

If you stay in the Holiday Inn at Preston today you'll be right in the background of
this shot and get a super view of Preston bus station. What you won't get is this
absolutely classic view of a Standerwick Leopard, in this case 942S, heading off for
London on a crisp winter's morn as the sun melts early frost. More's the pity.
David A. Powell

Above: Across the way I refer to 678 as being the first bus on the Alston-Haltwhistle rail-replacement service, on 3 May 1976. Here it is, two years later, descending from the highest point of England's highest market town, heading for Haltwhistle, inexcusably with no proper blind. Ribble worked with the local authorities to devise this route, which was much more accessible than the railway, then lost it in a tendering process. The end result would have been that Ribble's outstation in Alston and its one driver, taken over from United in 1969, would have been made redundant. The company appealed successfully, but my view of the local authorities, the Traffic Commissioners and the local press was forever tarnished. Ribble's was enhanced; they didn't have to do that, given the size of the company. Hence allowing the dire poppy red to make one of its few appearances in this tome. *John Howie*

Right: High up on Pendle Hill is the village of Barley, whence little Leopard 678, surrounded by the remnants of snow in November 1969, is departing to head back to Nelson. The bus claims to be going via Blacko, which is interesting enough, but the timetable claims Happy Valley, which sounds much more fun. Notwithstanding the driver's indifference, the service is believed to be a 280, another joint affair, this time with the Burnley, Colne & Nelson Joint Transport Board (itself an amalgam of three local authorities' transport departments). Seven years later 678 would be the first bus on Alston–Haltwhistle rail-replacement route 681. *Arnold Richardson / Photobus*

Above: Deepest Liverpool, and Burlingham-bodied PD3 1562 awaits a run out from Haymarket to Ford, a jointly operated route, in November 1971, with a distinctive green 'Corpy' bus behind. Ah, that's how things should be! It is a strange bus phenomenon that buses from big garages — and Ribble's Merseyside depots of Bootle and Aintree were really big — always seemed to sport a diesel stain by the filler cap. Maybe there were so many of them that the fuellers were always in a rush. Pity, because the bus is in fine form and by the fleetname style could not have been painted for some time. *Arnold Richardson / Photobus*

Right: The Town Hall in Carlisle, at the other end of the patch, was a focal point for Ribble's local services, which tended to ignore the bus station. Too right, for who would want to go there? A couple of PD3s led by 1570 wait by the splendid shelters in September 1969. It may have been a long way from Frenchwood, but Carlisle was important to Ribble. Indeed, three years later, in June 1972, the city services were converted to one-man operation with a revolutionary farebox system. It was pretty revolutionary in its lack of security too, but this is a family book. Nice flowers. *Arnold Richardson / Photobus*

Running from Wigan to Liverpool via St Helens and Abram, the 320 was a classic, being a joint operation between Ribble, Lancashire United Transport and Wigan and St Helens corporations, such that all shades of red could be seen thereon! PD2 1388 makes its way past an imposing church in Ashton-in-Makerfield on a sunny 11 July 1970 with a destination display that would make Major Hickmott — rightly a stickler for such things — turn in his grave. *Arnold Richardson / Photobus*

The 313 linked Chorley with Bolton via Westhoughton, where Leopard/Marshall 927 is seen in 1970. This was really bus work, but it demonstrates the versatility of dual-purpose vehicles and gives me pause to wonder why we don't have such things these days. Look, I know it's dirty, but to be fair this was December, so I think it can be forgiven. *Arnold Richardson / Photobus*

Left: What a spire! This one in Bury towers over second-generation 'White Lady' 1283 as she makes her way northwards to Skipton in October 1969. Of all Ribble's express services the X43 was particularly famous, and it is nice to see it still operating today under the prestige Witch Way brand adopted by the new Burnley & Pendle company. Again, although early Atlanteans, the 'White Ladies', new in 1962, put in 14-15 years' service. In their later lives they received bus livery and were unofficially known as 'Scarlet Women'. *Arnold Richardson / Photobus*

Right: This shot clearly shows how the 'Gay Hostess' coaches continued the tradition established by the postwar 'White Ladies' of clever use of trim to enhance what was basically a plain bus shell. Standerwick 27 here is posed outside Westminster Abbey in London having been hired by the Ribble Enthusiasts' Club to visit the 1968 Commercial Motor Show. The bald pate in the foreground belongs to none other than the Club's founder, the late T. B. Collinge. *Alan Haydock*

Left: Ribble's coaches could be found working express services in almost every corner of the UK. One of the major hubs was Cheltenham coach station, operated by Black & White Motorways. Mass departures took place several times a day to afford interchange; here, in July 1972, 869, a rather scruffy Plaxton-bodied Leopard, leaves to head back to Liverpool. Behind is typical Tilling fare, an ECW-bodied RE of Red & White. Next to 869 is arch-rival Midland Red's 6444, a splendid Willowbrook-bodied Leopard and one of a large fleet built up just prior to the scourge of the Leyland National (and the envy of many). But why didn't these fleets call themselves something sensible — after a river, for example?
Anthony Drury

Right: One of Ribble architect Cecil Quinn's finest achievements was the bus and coach station opened with great pomp and ceremony in Liverpool in 1960 after an expenditure of £190,000. This was on two levels, with buses on the lower level and coaches on the upper, from which Leopard/Harrington 721 is seen departing in 1968. Coach services, if anything, had more joint arrangements than did buses, involving numerous companies throughout Britain. No 721 here is setting off for Edinburgh on an X11 — one of a myriad of cross-border services to which Ribble was party. These were even more interesting in having different route numbers north and south of the border, and by the time it reaches 'Auld Reekie' 721 will have become a 501 in the Eastern Scottish company's numbering scheme. *Alan Haydock*

Left: Preston went from a rather ancient bus station to an ultra-modern one in 1969. Seen in the former in Tithebarn Street a year earlier is 1859, one of the strangely attractive Lowlanders unique to Ribble, if 16 buses can be unique. Memories will no doubt be stirred by the advertisement for the then all-dominant Players No 6 cigarettes. More obscure, but no doubt sadly missed locally, will be C&S XL ale. Not to worry; Preston can still turn out many a fine pint of the real stuff!
Alan Haydock

Above: Partway through its journey from Liverpool to Blackpool, Atlantean 1695 shows the slightly unusual combination of metal front fleetname plate and lower-case side fleetnames. Oops, bit heavy there; just enjoy this picture for the frankly scary vista of Preston bus station and a wonderful display of rear ends. Buses and coaches, that is; and amongst a fine Ribble array of the BET Federation's designs there's a nice Lancashire United Leopard/Plaxton. *David A. Powell*

Left: If it wasn't enough for the 561 on its twice-daily run (once on Saturdays and not at all on Sundays) to serve the wonderfully named Crosby Ravensworth, it also served Maulds Meaburn, where Leopard/Marshall 582, looking every inch a Ribble bus, has stopped at the timing point of High Stone Bridge in November 1970. So it must be 09.53. Oh, and it can't be a Tuesday because the 561 didn't run then either. Given the remoteness of the location, this is a reasonable load, justifying the oft-quoted description 'a rural lifeline'. *Arnold Richardson / Photobus*

Above: Look, this is a bus book, not a geography textbook, but I reckon Warrington was just about as far south as Ribble service buses got. Pause whilst those who favour such things as Ribble's southern cousin, Southdown, gulp at the words 'Warrington' and 'south' in the same sentence. Whatever, Atlantean 1626 sets off from Southport on a 309 towards Warrington on a journey that will skirt Liverpool passing through Winwick, Burtonwood, St Helens, Rainford, Skelmersdale and Ormskirk. If that were not enough, it was joint with St Helens Corporation and Lancashire United Transport. Not geography — history. *David A. Powell*

Left: Taking a day off from Liverpool locals, Bootle depot's PD2/Burlingham 1434 has worked an express to Skipton, which fair town it is about to depart to return to Liverpool. This route was more usually worked by single-deckers, so 1434 had probably been drafted in to provide extra capacity. *John Howie*

Left: A classic bit of Ribble operation in its heyday. This is an X14 Manchester–Morecambe express passing Robin Mill in Todmorden in 1970. But this Standerwick Leopard, 796S, is the duplicate; the service car is a Ribble 53-seat Leopard bus (534, if you want to be picky)! Things have to be done right, and although the company had been a Ribble subsidiary since 1932 the Standerwick coach very correctly carries an 'ON HIRE TO RIBBLE' sticker in its windscreen. Can you imagine a livery more beautifully adapted to the lines of this classic coach? Very soon such class, style and charisma would be subsumed beneath all-pervading National white. A crime, really. *David A. Powell*

Right: All too often neglected, the back of a bus. And in this case a design that was almost the epitome of the British double-decker in the 1950s and '60s — the MCW Orion. This lovely shot of PD2 1382 on a frosty morning in Burnley in November 1969 shows the detail of the type as fitted with platform doors (as well as demonstrating its incompatibility with nose-on bus stations). It also shows the family resemblance perpetuated, albeit with more upright profile, on the Atlantean alongside. And just look at the advertisements, the positive message about coaches long before low-cost airlines were thought of. But airlines are not ignored: note the advert for World travel and holidays — all available through Ribble, but not using 1382. *Arnold Richardson / Photobus*

Below: Cartmel is right in the middle of the Lakeland Peninsulas. It is famous for its Priory and for sticky toffee pudding. Some posh hotel in Windermere lays claim to that too, but, take my word for it, Cartmel takes some beating. Ribble provided an intricate network of services in this area, based in Grange-over-Sands and mainly taken over from the delightfully named Grange Motor & Cycle Company. The buses came in 1951, followed by the coaches in 1958; even in NBC days they were kept separate, drivers being allocated their own coach. With the Priory tower visible just above it, Leopard 569 approaches Cartmel in March 1970. *Arnold Richardson / Photobus*

Left: Close by the Turton & Entwhistle, Wayoh and Jumbles reservoirs, above Turton Bottoms and protected by Turton Tower, lies fair Edgeworth. Ribble's route 206 linked it with the metropolis of Bolton via Tonge Moor, and 898, a 1967 dual-purpose Marshall-bodied Leopard, is heading that way in this delightful autumnal scene from November 1971. The Americans call it 'fall', which is very descriptive, but doesn't 'autumn' just sum it up? *Arnold Richardson / Photobus*

Above: We've had lots of sunshine and autumnal tints; what about some slush? No 1645 was one of the first batch of Atlanteans delivered in 1960 and, despite problems with these buses, put in 16 years' service, which is good by any standards. It is seen here during the winter of 1973 in Walton, Liverpool, heading for Preston. *Richard Mellor*

31

Left: It's 6.30 on a Sunday morning, and the overnight Standerwick coaches, just arrived from London, are refuelling at Burnley before taking a well-earned rest before their next gruelling stint along the M6 and M1. A 'Gay Hostess' Atlantean follows on in this 1970 view. The refuelling bay, whilst not æsthetically pleasing, is notable for its practicality. The two standard Leopard/Plaxtons display the traditional metal fleetname (on the front) and the short-lived underlined transfer, both soon to be replaced by the lower-case version. *David A. Powell*

Above: Blimey! A Reliant Robin on 'L' plates (hogging the middle lane), a funny little caravan, no central-reservation crash barriers … can this really be the M6? Well, yes, of course it is, because there, in all its glory, is a Standerwick Plaxton Panorama-bodied Leopard, one of the first of a type to be forever linked with Ribble, out there in its spiritual home, the outside lane. In a move pandering to the perceptions/whims/prejudices (and votes) of the motorist, coaches have now been banned from such places. Is it any wonder that public transport is no longer so attractive? *David A. Powell*

Left: Now you associate Ribble and Lancashire with cotton mills, big built-up urban areas and so forth, don't you? Well, there's also a lot of very beautiful countryside in the Red Rose county, and Ribble looked after a lot of it. In far Dinckley, sort of near Whalley, between Clitheroe and Blackburn, we find 1666 ambling through the countryside looking for the latter. This was one of the first batch of Atlanteans, one of the semi-lowbridge type, that sent Ribble scurrying back to the PD3. Nevertheless, having entered service in June 1960, it was to put in a respectable 15 years before being disposed of in 1975. *Arnold Richardson / Photobus*

Right: Liverpool Pier Head in the early 1970s, and Ribble PD3/Metro-Cammell 1714 heads one of the Corporation's quirky Crossley-bodied PD2s, L262, in a scene recalling the great days of jointly operated public transport in the city. Mind you, the rot has set in, and signs of the Passenger Transport Executive, like all of them a 'nanny knows best' organisation doomed to destroy public transport by bureaucracy, are already evident in the form of the 'whirling wheel' symbol on the bus stop (clearly the wrong one). In a quaint throwback, 1714 carries logos promoting the BET — not Ribble's former owner, the British Electric Traction Co, but the Bus Economy Ticket. As Ribble buses carried letters only in the first line of their number blinds, routes such as the 55A could be shown only in reverse. Note the embossed fleetname on the radiator. Pride, huh? *David A. Powell*

Left: Just after this coach was delivered to Scout Motor Services in 1961 the company, which had worked closely (if not all that amicably) with Ribble, was taken over by its larger neighbour. Leopard/Duple (Midland) PRN 149 became S61, Scout initially retaining a separate identity, but by the time it was encountered at Seatoller in October 1968 it had become Ribble 1076. The frosted glass at the back denotes provision of a toilet — a rare facility for the time but necessary for the motorway service to London, of which Scout had a share. For Harrington 'affectionados', one of that builder's splendid coaches is behind. But most of all just look at those wonderfully autumnal Lakeland colours! *Arnold Richardson / Photobus*

Above: Scout Motor Services of Preston was a competitor of Ribble's for many years, but during World War 2 an uneasy truce was arranged. Thereafter things rubbed along, none too happily, until 1961, when Ribble took the company over. Differing operating practices saw Scout maintained as a separate entity until 1968, when it was fully absorbed, its buses being assimilated into the main fleet. Scout Atlantean/Metro-Cammell S1, later Ribble 1969, had semi-coach seating — useful, no doubt, for helping with Scout's share of the London services — and was unusual in being finished by Loughborough coachbuilder Willowbrook; maybe MCW wouldn't do it for fear of offending Ribble! Its registration was transferred to a private car when it was withdrawn in 1973, the bus being re-registered BTB 74A. Here it is a few years earlier in Blackburn. *David A. Powell*

Above: No 1688, one of the first batch of 95 Atlanteans, makes its way along stately Lord Street in Southport in July 1973, having arrived on the express service from Preston. Again, although not exactly welcomed with open arms by Ribble, this bus would manage a respectable 16 years of service. By now, however, the heyday was on the wane — it has NBC grey wheels. How tacky is that? *Arnold Richardson / Photobus*

Right: Big buses are very versatile. I remember once having a discussion with a pub landlord who was questioning my use of double-deckers past his rural watering-hole. I explained that they could carry two passengers or 72, and he saw the point. Ribble 1688 again makes the point as it wanders through rural Goosnargh, near Preston, on its way to Whittingham Hospital in July 1974 still with its grey wheels. *Arnold Richardson / Photobus*

Downham, nestling against the slope of Pendle Hill, enjoyed a remarkable Ribble service, the 215, via Clitheroe, Whalley, Blackburn and Darwen to Bolton. Even more remarkably, this was joint with Bolton Corporation, which was really rather a long way away. Passing through the autumnal tints of Dunscar as it nears Bolton in October 1971 is PD3 1511. *Arnold Richardson / Photobus*

Look at this idyllic scene — a wonderful display of flowers, rural peace and quiet …
where else could it be but suburban Bolton? PD3/Metro-Cammell 1758 sets off in
1973 on a short working to Blackburn on the 215 service. *David A. Powell*

Left: Ribble became a major player in Liverpool after its rather traumatic purchase of the Merseyside Touring Company (incidentally the owner of the area's largest bus, a massive 64-seater Tilling-Stevens) in 1930. Strange machinations forced Ribble to give up its recently acquired services to Liverpool Corporation, which wasn't that interested, but they came back to Ribble in 1933 after a spell with another company. This led to closer links with the 'Corpy', but Ribble drivers and guards (the proper Merseyside term for conductors) never really liked the urban work involved. PD2 1445 pulls away from a stop in Crosby in November 1971 before making its way via Seaforth Sands to Liverpool. The broken blind does said city an injustice. Unless you happen to be from Manchester. *Arnold Richardson / Photobus*

Above: Ribble's early experience with the Leyland Atlantean was not good, and very few of the original PDR model were purchased after the initial 95. By the mid-1970s, however, Leyland had sorted things out to produce the AN68, altogether a much better bus. This brought Ribble back, and a fleet of 186 was built up, 104 with this fabulous Park Royal body style. So, despite NBC livery and appalling destination screens, in my book these buses are part of Ribble's heyday. Even better, 1399 here is passing through Grasmere on the fantastic 555 route that passes through the heart of Lakeland. Hey, it is my book! *John Howie*

Above: Did you realise you could get Kentucky Fried Chicken in the late '60s? I didn't; I thought we only had Wimpy. This delightfully atmospheric shot of PD2/Burlingham 1435 coming off t' moors and dropping into Rawtenstall on an X43 from Burnley captures an aspect of Ribble operation to a 'T' (if not a 'KFC'). *David A. Powell*

Right: 'North of Diggle, south of Mumps, oop on t' moors where rain comes down in lumps'. So runs the ode, and this picture seems to sum it up. Except that it's not raining and miles away, at Belmont, near Bolton. The dual-purpose seems right as well, but strangely, with such an extensive network of express services, Ribble was very late into such things, taking its first only in 1964, following a change of General Manager. Leopard/Marshall 891, one of a batch of 14 DPs new in 1967, roars past a walker in September 1971. *Arnold Richardson / Photobus*

Left: The 291, linking Rawtenstall with Burnley, was worked jointly with Rawtenstall Corporation — one of a mind-numbing number of joint operating arrangements that kept a vast department at Frenchwood busy ensuring that every last penny was properly allocated. Ribble's first such arrangement was with nearby Haslingden Corporation, which, amalgamated with Rawtenstall, remains in municipal hands today as Rossendale Transport. Two days after Christmas in 1969, PD2 1382 passes through typical Lancashire surroundings in Crawshawbooth. The 291 also served Loveclough; I'll say no more. *Arnold Richardson / Photobus*

Above: Langdale probably sums up the Lake District — splendid scenery, good climbing, great pubs. It is also easily accessible year-round by service 516 from Ambleside to Dungeon Ghyll — one of the very few routes in Lakeland to be profitable. Elterwater, along the way, is delightful, and this splendid shot overcomes the fact that the bus is a poppy-red RESL/ECW. *John Howie*

Wigan was once home to two major bus bodybuilders — Massey and Northern Counties. In the '60s they amalgamated, and Northern Counties survived until the harsh times of the early 21st century. Their respective products are represented in this 1973 shot of a pair of Wigan Corporation Leyland Titans, 148 having a Massey body and the other NCME. The Ribble bus is interesting too, Alexander-bodied Lowlander 1968 being an ex demonstrator (and the only example south of the Scottish border badged as an Albion). Ribble took it over with Bamber Bridge Motor Services in 1967 after building up a fleet of 16 of its own, albeit with full-fronted bodywork. Service 352 was joint with Wigan and St Helens corporations.
David A. Powell

More usual Ribble fare — well, as far as Lowlanders go — is 1855, here in Wigan in 1973. It is passing Wigan Corporation No 40, an entirely local product featuring Massey bodywork on its Leyland PD2 chassis. The Ribble bus, unusually, differs considerably, being an all-Scottish product! All in all this is pretty much a heyday picture, with fabulous buildings and locally identified buses. All too soon Ribble's would be NBC poppy red, and Wigan's replaced by the dreadful, characterless orange of Greater Manchester PTE. *Richard Mellor*

Ribble revolutionised its coach fleet in 1951 with the introduction of 120 all-Leyland Royal Tiger coaches. Leyland established a special mass-production line for these vehicles, and all in all it was a pretty dramatic development, not only for Ribble but for the industry as a whole. They had the added and increasingly important advantage that two of the new coaches could carry the load of three of the earlier types and so brought welcome economy. This delightful picture in Burnley shows 894 with, presumably, local staff required to make it all happen.
Peter Yates collection

A Ribble coach; what more is there to say? Typical Plaxton-bodied Leopard 870 is pictured in Bolton in July 1972. Just look at those Lancashire stone setts. These were so prevalent in the company's area that, after trying Leyland's lightweight Olympic single-decker in 1950, Ribble reverted to the heavier Royal Tiger for most of its needs, building up a fleet of 110 that became synonymous with the fleet. For those of you who like them, one of the 49 Marshall-bodied Bristol RESLs can be seen in the background. *Arnold Richardson / Photobus*

Above: In a curious twist Ribble's northern outpost at Carlisle, an early user of highbridge double-deckers, went over to one-man operation in 1972 with a fleet of low-height double-deckers that were completely unnecessary for city services! Whilst most were new Bristol VRTs a selection of older lowbridge Atlanteans added spice; Metro-Cammell-bodied 1812 is seen here in the city centre on a damp and grimy day, offering a steamed-up-window return from shopping to the huge Morton Park estate. *David A. Powell*

Right: Now you may think this is in the wilds of Cheshire from the rather fine-timbered building on the right of the picture. But the bus gives it away. It's on the 236, linking Bolton with Burnley via Rawtenstall and typical of the sort of links Ribble provided between towns with their own municipal bus companies. What is a bit unusual is that the 236 wasn't jointly operated with anyone, although the fact that it passed through the territory of three bus-operating local authorities would have had a significant impact on fares, as Ribble aligned its fares with those of the municipalities, to be a suitable alternative for travellers. Atlantean 1687 passes through Holcombe, near Ramsbottom (home of yet another municipal operator), in November 1971. *Arnold Richardson / Photobus*

Above: In 1967 Skipton depot, known as the one in 'enemy territory' (Yorkshire), had five coaches, two 'White Lady' Atlanteans and three service buses, the last for its network of local bus services. Lined up outside the depot in Broughton Road is the entire service-bus allocation comprising two little Leopards and 1865, one of the 16 Alexander-bodied Lowlanders bought by Ribble during its 'disaffected with the Atlantean' years; odd-looking buses, they were in effect low-height PD3s and exuded a curious charm. In 1974 the local services passed to West Yorkshire Road Car, and subsequently the depot was sold to the much-respected (and still extant) Pennine Motor Services — yet another operator to run joint services with Ribble. *John Howie*

Right: Following its disappointment with its early Atlanteans Ribble returned to the type — this time the truly low-height PDR1/2 model — after experimenting with the Lowlander. The first 10, delivered in 1966, had Alexander bodies, as shown on page 62; the following year's delivery of 15 had Northern Counties bodywork. This was interesting, as, although based deep in Ribble territory at Wigan, Northern Counties had not previously been favoured in the company's orders. The design was one of the more successful on rear-engined double-deck chassis, managing to make what is essentially a box-like structure look more rounded, but sadly the PDR1/2s proved even more unhappy than had earlier Atlanteans. Despite this the Northern Counties buses became a familiar sight across the patch, Nos 1965/59/64 being seen huddled together inside Blackburn depot. *David A. Powell*

The X66 ran down the A666, linking Blackburn and Manchester via Darwen (which at this time had its own municipal bus company but was later to join Blackburn) and Bolton. It was another joint operation, this time with Lancashire United and those boys at Bolton Corporation again; they certainly seem to have been keen to be involved. It would be nice to be able to add 'and here's bus 666 working it', but 666 was a short Leopard based in Southport, so that would have been unlikely. Anyway 756, a 1964 Leopard/Plaxton, here in Bolton in January 1973, is much more the type of thing you would expect. When it and its sisters were introduced their panoramic windows were revolutionary and, so Ribble claimed, 'provided passengers with an unimpeded view of the passing countryside'. Or Bolton. The driver looks pretty fed up. *Arnold Richardson / Photobus*

The dreaming spires of … Lancaster. Leopard 548 was numerically the first of the 1964 Weymann-bodied batch — but why, as it wasn't delivered until February 1965, did it not receive a 'C'-suffix registration, as did, for example, 568 and 569, delivered the same month? Maybe because they were Marshall-bodied! Whatever, a lovely picture of Ribble in action. *David A. Powell*

Left: Two 'tanks' in Liverpool! The MCW-bodied PD3/5s were known universally by this name, but 1831 on the right is two and a half inches wider than 1772 on the left. Can you spot it? Both are in London Road, the apparent overprovision on the L3 to Crosby being explained by the fact that it is a one-way street, one bus having just left Skelhorne Street bus station whilst the other is just about to arrive!
Anthony Drury

Above: Appleby never really came to terms with the whole Cumbria thing and now styles itself as Appleby-in-Westmorland. It didn't need to in November 1970, when 663 was photographed gracing the Market Square, for at that time it still was in Westmorland. Ribble buses just plonked folk in the middle of the road, protected only by some white paint. A small (three-vehicle) outstation was maintained here in an old railway shed at the station, to which journeys were periodically extended for changeovers, parking and the like. And you thought it was a public-transport interchange. *Arnold Richardson / Photobus*

59

Ribble took the Bristol RE single-deck to its heart, and it has to be said the type was probably the best of a bad bunch of early rear-engined single-deckers. Forty of the longer RELL model were followed in 1971/2 by 89 of the shorter RESL type. Of these, 49 had Marshall bodies and sort of fitted in with Ribble's BET past, but the other 40 were pure Tilling in having ECW bodies. Still, they looked good in Ribble's traditional livery; here 345 emerges from Old Roan railway station in July 1974, having passed under the *raison d'être* for single-decks on the 54. Although technically joint with Merseyside PTE, Ribble ran this service. Nice BR sign. *Anthony Drury*

Now this isn't on; we all know that buses see a road sign pointing to their destination and go the other way! Bristol RE 223, here in tiny Rivington near the reservoir of the same name, has got this all wrong on a frosty morn in March 1969 and really is heading for Horwich from Chorley on a 312. If Ribble wasn't keen on Leyland's first-generation rear-engined double-deckers, it gave short shrift to its attempt at a single-deck version, taking just one Panther, in 1964. When the Bristol RE, a bus with a similar configuration, became available on the open market Ribble was a keen early user, although these first 10, dating from 1968, had Leyland engines. They also featured the then-fashionable dual-doorway layout — entirely unsuited to a route such as this! *Arnold Richardson / Photobus*

In 1966 Ribble took delivery of 10 low-height PDR1/2 Atlanteans with Alexander bodywork. This type of Atlantean was never a particularly happy bus, but many routes in East Lancashire required low double-deckers. By the late 1960s Blackburn was shedding its previous industrial image, and some nice green areas are to be seen beside the cathedral as 1873 arrives from Preston via Ribchester in company with some rather fine estate cars of the day. *John Howie*

Ribble readily embraced the newly authorised width of 8ft, between 1948 and 1950 buying more than 200 Leyland PD2s to this width, many with Leyland's own bodywork. The company was less dynamic over the much more comfortable highbridge design, sticking mainly to the lowbridge layout, and the final 30 all-Leyland PD2s, delivered in 1952, stuck to that arrangement. Nevertheless they were splendid buses, perhaps the embodiment of the heyday of British bus-building. Here 1377 waits in Rochdale before returning to Preston. *Arnold Richardson / Photobus*

Above: A major British city — Liverpool — in 1973, and look at how folk still manage to walk about without all the urban clutter of today. Are the family with the suitcases about to embark upon their important holiday (hopefully, as 1579 urges, booked with Ribble)? Will they partake of a meal, snack, pie or sandwich from the Punch & Judy or settle down in the Buttery of the St George Hotel? Buttery? Such things are long gone … as is 1579, working a 'Skem' short on the 201 from Liverpool to Upholland. *David A. Powell*

Right: Occasionally a 561 would wander through vast empty tracts of what was Westmorland to link Kendal and Appleby via Crosby Ravensworth. Slightly more frequently it went as far as Tebay, where 674 is seen in November 1970. Another of the 'little Leopards' of 1966, the bus is crossing the remote valley that was once home only to the railway but which had just gained the M6 motorway and a service area, thus becoming rather less remote. A new bridge is visible in the background. That's almost certainly the driver taking a passenger's shopping on board — typical of this type of operation, despite its being part of a vast organisation. *Arnold Richardson / Photobus*

Above: This is Ribble red. In these days when wine, beer, malt whisky, all manner of things are subjected to in-depth tasting notes, how would we describe this? 'Deep red with a hint of plum, offset with just the right amount of creamy waistrail'? Ah, just plain classy does it for me. 'Tank' 1723 in Morecambe works a 570 linking Lancaster with Morecambe and Heysham — a route known to crews as 'The Track'. In the background is a Morecambe & Heysham Corporation Pennine-bodied AEC Swift, a type of bus Ribble would never have considered — which just goes to show how interesting buses were in the 1960s and early '70s. *David A. Powell*

Right: Grizedale Forest is a largely unknown part of the Lake District, and right in the middle of it is Grizedale itself with its Hall. Ulverston depot was charged with bringing the village children to the school in Spark Bridge, the timetable ominously advising that the service was 'liable to suspension if not so required'. During school holidays, however, a full-blown off-peak service on the 510 operated right through to Ulverston. Twice a day. On Thursdays. Leopard 587 passes through Force Forge in November 1969. *Arnold Richardson / Photobus*

Ribble's useful long-distance routes, linking many centres of population, gradually became victims of disruption owing to traffic congestion. Reluctantly the company embarked on a policy of cutting them, thus reducing choice and increasing costs but hopefully delivering better reliability; for this reason the 150, which used to link Burnley and Blackburn with Morecambe, was cut short at Preston. In autumnal sunlight (that fails to disguise its NBC grey wheels!) Atlantean 1632 makes its way along Preston New Road in Blackburn in 1973. Note the lack of other traffic! *David A. Powell*

One of Ribble's more remote outposts was Knott End on Sea, where this gorgeous 1956 PD2, 1441, with Burlingham bodywork built not too far away in Blackpool, is seen arriving after a wander across the flat land from said resort, having served Poulton and Hambleton on the way. A nice display of roses, no doubt aided by July 1970 sunshine, nestles up to a typical piece of architecture of the time. I don't suppose the gardener ever gave 1441 and its ilk a passing glance. Had it been me … well, the roses would have withered. *Arnold Richardson / Photobus*

Ribble had always supported local products, witness its close association with Leyland Motors. When Leyland stopped building bus bodies there was a sort of understanding that its customers went to MCW in Birmingham for their double-deck needs. Ribble was one such, but, joy of joys, also went to nearby Burlingham of Blackpool in 1956 for some of the most stylish rear-entrance buses ever to grace Britain's streets. There were 45 of them, and they incorporated a special type of platform door — the 'Southlanco' — which slid into the bodywork, giving more circulating space on the platform. Well, all bar the last five did. (Who knows why? I certainly don't.) No 1468, descending into Blackburn, shows the doors cross-checked and closed. *David A. Powell*

When we lost Arnold Richardson in 2005, the enthusiast fraternity — indeed, the industry itself — lost a true giant. Many pictures in this book are Arnold's, but this one I dedicate to his memory. The 514 linked Ulverston with Cunsey Road End, in Grizedale Forest, but twice a day on Thursdays only. On 14 March 1970 Arnold travelled the route, taking no fewer than 14 pictures of Leopard 589 to record this remote outpost of British bus operation. I was spoiled for choice but chose this one, as here, at Lakeside, is to be found the terminus of both the Windermere boats and the Lakeside & Haverthwaite Railway. Thank you, Arnold. *Arnold Richardson / Photobus*

"Ee oop, there's another in theer!" quips the man in brown. Ribble bought the old Cheshire Lines Committee railway station in Southport for £72,500 in 1953, opening it on 25 June 1954 as what must have been one of the UK's whackiest bus stations. Metro-Cammell-bodied 1793 heads a line of PD3s waiting for duty within the confines of what could only have been a railway station. Note the posters advertising day trips to the Isle of Man for £2.20; although these imply travel by ferry Ribble was an early user (in 1951) of the Blackpool–Ronaldsway air service and by 1958 could claim its 100,000th passenger on the link. *David A. Powell*

The first coaches ordered by Ribble (as opposed to diverted from Scout) to the new maximum length of 36ft arrived in 1963. They were handsome Harrington-bodied Leopards seating 49; 709 here is reversing off the old Preston bus station in 1967 partway through a Keswick–Manchester run. *David A. Powell*

Fleetwood was a Ribble area on Merseyside with its own network of local services. The F1 here reflected the seasonal nature of the place by being extended to serve the Rossall Lane Camp during the summer and may well still be doing that in this early

September 1969 view of Burlingham-bodied PD3 1540. The chap on the right doesn't need 1540 — he's got his fine Vauxhall Cresta. You can lean on it too, unlike a PD3. *Arnold Richardson / Photobus*

The 36ft 53-seat Leopard buses became a Ribble trademark and earned themselves the unofficial title of 'Red Setters'. Numbering 190 vehicles, they could be seen all over the company's patch. Bodywork was standard to the BET style although built by Metro-Cammell, Weymann and Marshall. Ribble claimed to have had a hand in the design; whatever, it is a classic and still looks sleek and modern today. A very much in-service Marshall-bodied 529 shows off this style icon at Chorley bus station in March 1973. *Anthony Drury*

Left: If it looks as if there is nobody on this bus then that's probably right. Given that some of the stuff that survived the cull of the early '70s carried very little, that which went must have been dire. The 563, linking Ulverston with Seathwaite, way up the remote Duddon Valley, didn't last long after little Leopard 665 was working it in March 1970. *Arnold Richardson / Photobus*

Above: By a nifty piece of footwork in 1931 in buying up seven of the 14 small bus companies therein, Ribble came from behind amongst the larger companies in the city of Carlisle to become the major player. When the city's trams ceased in that year, Ribble became the dominant operator, and the city became an important northern outpost of the empire. On a quiet May day in 1969 PD2 1401 waits to go to Botcherby on a route recently taken over from United. Ribble later extended it into the huge Harraby estate. *Arnold Richardson / Photobus*

Above: Just north-west of Kendal are some delightful villages strung out through fabulous South Lakeland scenery. Often overlooked in the mad dash for more famous parts, they for many years enjoyed the services of the 541, which linked Kendal to Underbarrow, Brigsteer, Crosthwaite and Dawson Fold before ending up at Low Farm in the Lyth Valley. Sadly they were overlooked by passengers too, and the service was severely cut back soon after 219 was pictured turning at Brigsteer in May 1970. *Arnold Richardson / Photobus*

Right: There's a lot of the Leeds & Liverpool Canal in Burscough Bridge for PD2 1424 to cross in October 1969. There's a railway too. Having started in Liverpool, heading out through Maghull and Ormskirk, the bus is bound for Blackburn, with still Chorley to cross before it reaches its destination on the 331. Notice how all the advertisements promote Ribble products, from coaches linking most towns in Britain to worldwide travel. *Arnold Richardson / Photobus*

Atlantean 1688 clearly shows off Ribble red as it enters Lancaster bus station on its way from Preston to Morecambe on the trunk 140 route. Every inch a Ribble bus in its heyday! Just look at those telephone boxes; do you remember when individual boxes were sited so close together? And they were used! Ring me on my mobile and let me know. *David A. Powell*